Afternoon Tea

at the

Arboretum

Afternoon Tea

at the

Arboretum

Judy Scott

Brown Books Publishing Group
Dallas, Texas

Afternoon Tea at the Arboretum
©2010 Judy Scott

For information, please contact:

Brown Books Publishing Group
16200 North Dallas Parkway, Suite 170
Dallas, Texas 75248

www.brownbooks.com

972-381-0009

ISBN-13: 978-1-934812-64-8
ISBN-10: 1-934812-64-1

LCCN:2010920709
1 2 3 4 5 6 7 8 9 10

My daughter, Jennifer

Dedication

This book is dedicated to my family.
When I asked for help, they were there for me
(even washing dishes). I love you all.

My grandson, Dylan

My son, Daniel, his wife, Kim, and their
children, Ryan and Ashley

My great-granddaughter, Maya

My grandchildren, Krystal and Michael

My son, Greg

My son, Michael, and his wife, Donna

Contents

Acknowledgments

Special thanks to Mary Brinegar, the president of the Dallas Arboretum, for her faith and encouragement and for guiding us in orchestrating the ambiance of the tea, finding solutions when needed, and making the tea experience a great success.

R.W. Nelson, thank you for being such a great asset to the tea and for making everyone feel special.

Darryl Delk, for your loyalty and dedication since the beginning, you have my sincere thanks.

Tony Villagomez, thank you for giving me your best and keeping us all cool and composed.

Thanks to my outstanding kitchen staff for keeping the flow going so the tea went smoothly.

Quita Bartholomew, my right hand—thank you for taking reservations at the Arboretum and helping with the seating arrangements.

Last, but not least, I extend my gratitude to Judith Jenkins and Martin Mendoza, without whose creativity and undivided devotion none of this would have been possible.

Special recognition and love goes to Donna Scott, my daughter-in-law, who spent hours turning pictures and recipes into an actual cookbook.

All About Tea

The English began drinking tea in the late 1650s. As both the brewed beverage and the dry loose leaves were extremely expensive, it immediately became the drink of the royal family and the aristocracy. We cannot be certain of the exact origin of the Afternoon Tea, but one lady is featured in every theory—Anna, Seventh Duchess of Bedford, lady-in-waiting to her majesty, Queen Victoria.

Traditionally, dinner was not served until 8:30 or 9:00 in the evening, and the Duchess often became hungry before dinner. One afternoon, she ordered a small meal of bread, butter, cakes, tarts, and biscuits to be brought secretly to her boudoir. These refreshments satisfied her so well that she ordered them again the next day and every afternoon thereafter.

In the late 1800s "taking tea" became so popular that hotels began to offer tea service in tea courts. Since it was socially unacceptable for unmarried men and women to be seen with each other alone, these tea rooms became places where they could meet for tea and conversation. Today, the idea is that men are not expected to come to tea, but in the 1800s that was not the case; men accompanied their ladies.

High Tea is served around 6:00 PM and is a hearty evening meal, not to be confused with the Afternoon Tea that consists of dainty sandwiches, cakes, pastries, and scones served in elegant surroundings.

How to brew tea :

Fill teapots with hot water.
Empty the teapots.
Add loose leaf tea (2 tablespoons per pot).
Fill with hot water and let sit for 15 minutes.
Put a tea strainer over a cup and pour the tea.
Never boil tea.

Afternoon Tea Menu
Degolyer Garden Café—Dallas Arboretum

First Course
Tomato Herb Broth with Cheese Wafer

Second Course
Tea Sandwiches
Banana Nut Bread with Cream Cheese Center
Turkey with Herb Butter on Rosemary Bread
Egg Salad on Onion Bread
Tarragon Chicken Salad with Apples and Pecans on Croissant

Third Course
Pecan Tarts
Flower Sugar Cookies
Amaretto Brownies
Chocolate Dipped Strawberries
Lemon Bars
Orange Currant Scones with Strawberry Jam and Clotted Cream

Tea Selections
Apricot Orange, Orange Spice Decaf, Strawberry Vanilla,
Peach Ginger, Darjeeling

Afternoon Tea

Tomato Herb Broth

Ingredients

Makes one gallon of broth. Freeze in quarts to use later. Serve hot!

2 46-ounce cans tomato juice

1/2 cup chopped onions

1/2 cup sliced green onions

2 tablespoons dill weed

1/2 teaspoon cumin

1 1/2 quarts water

1 1/4 cups chopped celery

1/4 cup chicken base

1/4 teaspoon ground cloves

Directions

Mix these ingredients well.

Chill thoroughly for 24 hours before serving to let the flavors blend.

Cheese Wafers

Ingredients

- 1/2 lb margarine or butter
- 4 cups grated cheddar cheese
- 2 cups flour
- 1 cup finely chopped pecans
- 1 tablespoon paprika
- 1 teaspoon cayenne pepper

Directions

Blend margarine and cheese. Add flour. Mix until blended. Add pecans, paprika, and cayenne. Blend.

Roll into 2-inch diameter rolls. Wrap rolls in plastic wrap and chill.

Slice into 1/4-inch slices.

Bake at 350° until crisp (10–15 minutes).

Butternut Squash Soup

A most delicious soup for fall

Ingredients

Makes 4 to 5 cups

1 tablespoon low fat vegetable oil spread

1 tablespoon minced shallots or onions

2 cloves minced garlic or 1 teaspoon chopped garlic

3 sprigs fresh thyme

1/4 teaspoon dried rosemary or 1/2 teaspoon fresh rosemary

2 packages (10 ounces each) frozen butternut squash thawed or 1 1/2 lbs cooked butternut squash (fresh is definitely better). To cook fresh, cut in half and remove seeds. Bake on oiled cookie sheet until done—about 20–30 minutes. Remove skin and mash.

3 tablespoons skim milk

1 cup fat free, low sodium chicken broth

1/2 cup canned pumpkin

1/2 teaspoon cinnamon

1/2 teaspoon white pepper

Sour cream

Salt to taste

Directions

Melt vegetable spread in medium saucepan over medium heat. Add shallots, garlic, thyme, and rosemary. Cook, stirring 2–3 minutes or until aromatic.

Stir in squash and bring to a boil. Add milk and chicken broth. Add pumpkin. Add more broth if needed.

Remove thyme sprigs. Transfer soup to blender or food processor and process until smooth.

Add cinnamon, salt, and white pepper.

Heat and serve with a dollop of sour cream if desired.

Egg Salad

Ingredients

  8 hard-boiled eggs
  3/4 cup mayonnaise
  1 celery stalk, chopped fine
  3 green onions, chopped fine (include both tops
    and bottoms)
  Salt and white pepper to taste

Directions

  Incorporate egg whites and egg yolks (a fork works well for this—or a pastry blender).

  Add celery and onions. Combine salt and pepper with mayonnaise; add mayonnaise until ingredients stick together.

  Always use while fresh, within 2 days.

Marge's Cucumber Sandwiches

Ingredients

Make early in the day; spread sets for a few hours.

1 cup celery, finely chopped
1/2 cup green pepper, finely chopped
1 small onion, finely chopped
2 cucumbers, peeled, seeded, and coarsely grated
Unflavored gelatin (one package)
2 cups mayonnaise
Frozen, thin-sliced white bread (crusts removed)

A food processor may be used for all vegetables. Save juice.

Directions

After coarsely grating the cucumbers (not very coarse), lightly salt and let stand a few minutes (it takes at least 30 minutes to make juice). Add all juice to one package unflavored gelatin. Heat to melt gelatin.

Add 2 cups regular mayonnaise and finely chopped vegetables. Let harden in refrigerator. Spread on frozen, thin sliced white bread, crusts removed. Place in airtight container in refrigerator.

These are just as good, and do not get soggy, if made two days before. Spread bread generously with filling and cut into sections.

Chicken Tarragon Salad

Ingredients

Makes 4 cups of salad or about 8 sandwiches

2 cups cooked chicken breast, chopped

2 celery stalks, chopped

1 large red apple, peeled and chopped

1 cup chopped pecans

1 tablespoon dried tarragon

1 cup mayonnaise

Salt to taste

Directions

Mix all ingredients well. Let stand in refrigerator 1–8 hours to let the flavors blend.

Delicious on mini croissants, banana bread, or strawberry bread for tea sandwiches.

Banana Bread

Ingredients

Makes 4 loaves

3 cups sugar
1 cup butter
4 eggs
1/2 cup milk
4 cups flour
2 teaspoons baking soda
2 teaspoons vanilla
6 very ripe bananas, mashed
1 cup chopped pecans

Directions

Preheat oven to 325°.

Blend sugar and butter together. Add the eggs one at a time. Add vanilla with milk. Mix in flour and baking soda, then add bananas. Mix well. Add pecans.

Divide into four medium loaf pans prepared with baking spray so the bread will not stick. Bake for 75 minutes, or until toothpick comes out clean. This makes a light-colored bread.

Strawberry Bread

Ingredients

Use fresh or whole frozen strawberries

3 cups all-purpose flour

1 teaspoon salt

2 cups sugar

1 1/4 cups vegetable oil

1 teaspoon baking soda

1 teaspoon cinnamon

4 eggs, beaten

2 cups sliced strawberries

1 1/4 cups chopped pecans

Directions

Combine dry ingredients. Add eggs, oil, strawberries, and pecans. Stir just until all ingredients are moistened.

Scrape batter into two well greased 9 x 5 x 3-inch loaf pans. Bake at 350° for 60–70 minutes, or until a toothpick inserted comes out clean.

Cool in pans 5 minutes, then remove and cool on a wire rack. Sprinkle with powdered sugar if desired or slice and, when cooled, spread with cream cheese or chicken salad for tea sandwiches.

Spritz Cookies

Ingredients

These cookies were used as our cutout cookies for the tea. Cookies can be stored in airtight containers.

2 cups (4 sticks) butter (room temperature)
1 1/2 cups sugar
4 egg yolks
2 teaspoons vanilla
3 1/2 cups flour

Directions

Cream butter and sugar. Add egg yolks and vanilla. Add flour.

Lightly flour board and place mixture on board. Roll dough like pie crust and cut into shapes for specific holidays, or put mixture in cookie press and press out cookies.

Bake at 325° for 12–15 minutes. Cool 5 minutes and remove from cookie sheet. When cool, cover with icing and decorate.

My grandmother made these cookies every holiday.

Pumpkin Bread

Ingredients

Makes 4 medium loaves

3 cups sugar
1 1/2 cups brown sugar
1 1/2 cups oil
5 cups canned pumpkin
6 eggs
6 cups flour
1 tablespoon baking soda
1/2 tablespoon salt
1/2 tablespoon nutmeg
1/2 tablespoon ginger
3/4 cup water
1 1/2 cups seedless raisins
1 cup chopped pecans

Directions

Mix together sugar, brown sugar, oil, canned pumpkin, eggs, and water. In a separate bowl, mix flour, baking soda, salt, nutmeg, and ginger. Combine wet and dry ingredients. Add raisins and pecans.

Divide between 4 medium loaf pans. Bake at 325° until toothpick inserted in center comes out clean—about 1 hour.

Scones

Ingredients

Makes 18 scones. Freeze dough and bake a few scones at a time.

1/4 cup unsalted butter (1/2 stick)
2 3/4 cups flour
1 tablespoon sugar
1 teaspoon baking powder
1/4 teaspoon baking soda
1/2 cup heavy whipping cream
1 egg beaten
1/2 cup dried cranberries or currants
1 orange zest (grated orange rind)
1 1/2 tablespoons orange juice

Directions

Mix flour, sugar, baking powder, and baking soda. Cut in butter with fork or pastry blender until blended. Add cranberries or currants (soaked in orange juice) and orange zest. Add heavy whipping cream whipped with egg.

Mix until dough will separate from bowl. Do not overmix. Turn out on lightly floured board. Roll or pat to 1/2-inch thickness. Cut with floured 2-inch round cutter. Place on ungreased cookie sheet. Bake at 350° for 15–20 minutes.

Devonshire Clotted Cream

Directions

Whip 1/2 cup of whipping cream.
Add 1 cup sour cream and Devonshire powder.
Stir until blended.

(Devonshire powder can be ordered on the Internet.)

Appetizers and Party Drinks

Hot Crab Parmesan Artichoke Dip

Ingredients

- 1 tablespoon vegetable oil
- 1 green bell pepper (remove seeds, chop, and sauté in the oil)
- 1 14-ounce can artichoke hearts (drained and chopped fine)
- 1 cup mayonnaise
- 1/4 cup thinly sliced scallions
- 1/2 cup grated Parmesan cheese
- 3/4 tablespoon lemon juice
- 2 teaspoons Worcestershire sauce
- 1/2 teaspoon celery salt
- 8 ounces crab meat, drained (more if desired)
- 1/3 cup toasted sliced almonds
- Toasted pita bread triangles

Directions

Combine all ingredients except crab meat and almonds. Gently stir in crab meat.

Pour into buttered baking dish and sprinkle with almonds. Bake at 375° for 25–30 minutes. Triangles can be used to dip hot crab.

Festive Appetizer Spread

Ingredients

1 cup water
1 cup sugar
12 ounces fresh or frozen cranberries
1/2 cup apricot preserves
2 tablespoons lemon juice
1/3 cup toasted slivered almonds
1 8-ounce package cream cheese
Assorted crackers

Directions

Combine water and sugar in saucepan. Boil without stirring for 5 minutes. Add cranberries and cook until they pop and sauce is thickened, about 10 minutes. Remove from heat.

Cut the apricots in the preserves into small pieces. Add to cranberry mixture. Stir in lemon juice. Cool and add almonds. Spoon over cream cheese.

Hot Crab Dip

Ingredients

Makes about 3 1/2 cups

8 ounces cream cheese, softened
1/4 cup sour cream
2 cloves garlic, minced (about 1 teaspoon)
1/4 cup finely chopped onion
2 tablespoons Worcestershire sauce
1 1/2 teaspoons Dijon mustard
2 teaspoons prepared horseradish
1 teaspoon lemon juice
1 lb crab meat, flaked and picked through to remove any shells or cartilage
Salt and pepper to taste
2 tablespoons freshly grated Parmesan cheese

Directions

Preheat oven to 350°.

Mix together cream cheese, sour cream, garlic, onion, Worcestershire sauce, mustard, horseradish, and lemon juice. Add crab meat, salt, and pepper; combine well.

Place in a lightly greased 1 1/2-quart baking dish. Sprinkle with the Parmesan cheese. (Can be prepared several hours ahead and refrigerated until baking.) Bake until hot and bubbly, 20–30 minutes. Cool about 5 minutes before serving.

Note: Both Worcestershire sauce and Dijon mustard are salty, so go easy on the salt. The mixture will appear very thick when cold but will thin out during baking. Add a little milk if you prefer a thinner spread. You may keep the dip hot on a chafing dish when serving or just let it stand at room temperature. If desired, reheat in microwave.

Variations: Sprinkle top with sliced almonds or chopped pecans before baking. Substitute cheddar cheese for the Parmesan. Garnish top with chopped parsley or paprika for color.

Teresa's Cheese Ball

Ingredients

Makes 1 1/2 lb cheese ball

2 8-ounce packages cream cheese
1 8-ounce package thin sliced ham, chopped
3 green onions, chopped (include tops)
1 1/2 teaspoons Accent®
1/2 teaspoon cayenne pepper
1/2 teaspoon garlic powder
1/2 teaspoon onion salt
1/2 teaspoon Worcestershire sauce

Directions

Mix cream cheese, ham, onion, Accent®, cayenne pepper, garlic powder, onion salt, and Worcestershire sauce. Roll into a ball with your hands and cover with chopped pecans. Chill and serve with crackers.

Texas Caviar

Favorite recipe from Bob Hildee

Ingredients

32-ounce bag frozen kernel corn, thawed
1 cup sour cream
1 cup mayonnaise
8 ounces grated cheddar cheese
8 ounces grated Monterrey jack cheese
8 ounces jalapeño, chopped
1 large can chopped green chilies
1 small can chopped black olives
1 small jar chopped pimentos
1 jalapeño, chopped fine
2 green onions, chopped
1 poblano chili

Directions

Place the poblano chili in a heavy pan or in the oven and char so that the skin peels off. Cut in half and remove seeds; then chop fine.

Mix together all ingredients, cover and let sit in the refrigerator at least an hour. Serve with chips or crackers.

Fresh Cranberry Relish

Ingredients

This is a colorful and delicious side dish. No matter how much I make, they want more.

4 cups cranberries (16-ounce package)
2 apples, cored
2 oranges, seeded
Orange zest
3/4 cup sugar

Directions

Zest oranges. Chop cranberries, peel and chop cored apples, and chop peeled and seeded oranges. Mix together with all the juices from the fruits. Add sugar.

Poppy Seed Dressing

Ingredients

The secret is in the mixing.

2 cups vegetable oil
1 1/2 cups sugar
2/3 cups white vinegar
3 tablespoons poppy seeds
3 tablespoons onion juice
2 teaspoons dry mustard
2 teaspoons salt

Directions

Combine sugar, vinegar, dry mustard, onion juice, and salt. Add oil very slowly on medium speed until mixture is thick. Add poppy seeds and beat 2 seconds.

Makes about 1 1/2 pints. It will keep in the refrigerator for about one month. Stir before serving.

Great for fruit salad, mixed greens, or spinach salads.

Roquefort Grapes

Ingredients

These cheese-coated grapes can also be rolled in chopped unroasted pistachio or macadamia nuts. They may be made up two days in advance and kept refrigerated in an airtight container. Any leftover cheese mixture can be frozen.

10 ounces almonds, pecans, or walnuts
8 ounces cream cheese at room temperature
4 ounces Roquefort cheese at room temperature
2 tablespoons heavy cream
1 lb (about 48) red or green seedless grapes

Directions

Heat oven to 300°.

Spread the nuts evenly on a rimmed baking sheet and bake until lightly toasted and aromatic, 8–12 minutes. Cool slightly.

Chop the toasted nuts coarsely in a food processor or by hand. Transfer to a platter and spread out evenly.

In the bowl of an electric mixer, combine the cream cheese, Roquefort cheese, and cream and beat on low speed until smooth, 2–3 minutes.

Drop clean, dry grapes into the loose cheese mixture. Use a rubber spatula to stir the grapes in the mixture until each grape is coated. Working one at a time, transfer the grapes to the chopped nuts and roll the grapes in the nuts until they are well coated.

Transfer the grapes to a rimmed baking sheet lined with parchment paper or wax paper. Cover with plastic wrap and refrigerate until serving.

Plantation Tea

From Nell Denman

Ingredients

6 cups boiling water
5 regular tea bags
3/4 cup lemon juice
1 1/2 cups sugar
1 cup pineapple juice
2 cups ginger ale

Directions

Brew tea, remove tea bags, and add other remaining ingredients.

Wassail

Ingredients

Makes about 32 servings

1 gallon apple cider
2/3 cup sugar
2 teaspoons whole cloves
2 teaspoons whole allspice
2 three inch sticks cinnamon
2 oranges studded with cloves

Directions

Heat all ingredients except oranges. Strain and put in bowl. Float oranges.

Champagne Punch

Ingredients

Makes approximately 5 quarts

2 cups sugar

2 cups water

Juice of 6 lemons

2 cups apricot nectar

1 6-ounce can frozen orange juice

2 12-ounce cans apple juice

2 cups pineapple juice

2 12-ounce bottles ginger ale

2 fifths champagne

Directions

Boil sugar and water for 1 minute. Cool. Add juices. Freeze. Thaw 1 to 1 1/2 hours before serving. Add ginger ale and champagne.

Serve over circle of ice in punch bowl. (Freeze a few pieces of sliced fruit in a ring mold.)

Light Lunches

How to cook chicken:

Any time cooked chicken is called for, cook it with this recipe.

6 chicken breasts
3 carrots cut into large pieces
4 ribs of celery cut into pieces
1 large onion cut into quarters
Salt

Place all ingredients in large pan. Cover with water and bring to boil. Cook until chicken is tender. Do not over-cook! Keep cover on saucepan.

Remove carrots, celery, and onion and put ice cubes in the broth to remove fat. Strain.

You can pour the broth into plastic ice cube trays and place in plastic bags when frozen. Use as needed to flavor vegetables, or use for soup.

Broccoli Cheese Soup

Ingredients

1 package frozen chopped broccoli
2 10-ounce cans cream of mushroom soup
1 can evaporated milk
8 ounces shredded Colby cheese
1 small box Velveeta® cheese, cubed or sliced
Salt and pepper to taste

Directions

Boil broccoli and drain. In a large pan, combine soup with milk. Add Velveeta® and heat until melted. Add broccoli, salt, and pepper.

Serve in bowls, and garnish with Colby cheese.

Ingredients

Variation:
1 quart chicken stock
2 heads fresh broccoli, chopped fine
2 medium onions, chopped
1 lb Velveeta® cheese, cut into chunks
Salt and pepper to taste

Directions

Mix together stock, broccoli, and onion in large pan and cook on low heat—approximately 30 minutes. Add salt, pepper, and Velveeta®; stir until cheese is melted.

Serve at once.

Gazpacho

Ingredients

Serves 8

Gazpacho soup was created for the summer. Refreshingly cold on hot summer days, this adaptation of the classic Spanish cold tomato soup deliciously combines the best of summer vegetables. Make sure you only use the freshest, highest quality ingredients for this soup.

6 ripe tomatoes, peeled and chopped

1 purple onion, finely chopped

1 cucumber (or more), peeled, seeded and chopped

2 stalks celery, chopped

1–2 tablespoons chopped fresh parsley

2 tablespoons chopped fresh chives

1 clove garlic, minced

1/4 cup red wine vinegar

1/4 cup olive oil

2 tablespoons freshly squeezed lemon juice

2 teaspoons sugar

Salt and fresh ground pepper to taste

6 or more drops of Tabasco® sauce to taste

1 teaspoon Worcestershire sauce (omit for vegetarian option)

4 cups tomato juice

Directions

Combine all ingredients. Blend, slightly, to desired consistency. Place in non-metal, non-reactive storage container, cover tightly, and refrigerate overnight, allowing flavors to blend.

Tomato Basil Soup

Ingredients

2 large onions, chopped

1/2 cup butter

2 cups diced tomatoes

5 cups chicken broth

1 50-ounce can tomato soup

3 cups milk

1 tablespoon dry basil

1/2 cup brown sugar

1/4 teaspoon dry oregano

1/4 teaspoon thyme

Salt and pepper to taste

Parmesan cheese

Croutons

Directions

Sauté onions in butter. Add remaining ingredients and bring to boil. Garnish with grated Parmesan cheese and croutons if desired.

Potato Soup

Ingredients

Makes 1 gallon

1 cup yellow onions, diced
1 carrot, grated
1/2 cup flour
1 gallon chicken broth
6 cups mashed potatoes
5 slices crisp bacon, chopped
3 cups chopped green onions
6 cups diced potatoes
4 cups milk
2 tablespoons butter
White pepper and salt to taste

Directions

Sauté onions in butter. Add flour. Add remaining ingredients one at a time. Heat on medium until potatoes are done.

Serve at once. Garnish with grated cheese if desired.

Soup can be frozen for later use.

World's Best Clam Chowder

Ingredients

1 12-ounce can clams
1 cup chopped onions
1 cup chopped celery
3 cups diced potatoes
1/4 cup butter
1/4 cup flour
2 cups half-and-half
2 cups milk
1 1/2 teaspoons salt
1/2 teaspoon granulated sugar
1/2 teaspoon vinegar
2 strips of crisp bacon, chopped

Directions

Drain juice from clams and pour over potatoes. Add enough water to cover. Cook for about 10 minutes; add sugar, vinegar, and salt. Cook until potatoes are tender.

Melt butter; sauté celery and onions. Add flour and blend. Add half-and-half and milk, stirring constantly. Add potatoes (do not drain) and mix thoroughly. Add clams. Garnish with crisp bacon.

Black Bean Salad

Ingredients

Makes 4 cups

2 cans black beans
1 cup diced tomatoes
1 cup diced celery
1/4 cup red onion

Directions

Mix all with vinaigrette dressing (just enough to moisten).
Add whole kernel corn if desired.

Broccoli Salad

Ingredients

Serves 10

3/4 cup mayonnaise

1/4 cup sugar (or 2 packages Splenda®)

1 1/2 tablespoons soy sauce

4 tablespoons red wine vinegar

2 12-ounce bags broccoli florets (about 8 cups)

1 cup golden raisins or dried cranberries

1/2 cup coarsely chopped pecans, toasted

1/2 cup sliced green onion

1 11-ounce can mandarin oranges, drained (optional)

Directions

In a small mixing bowl, whisk together the mayonnaise, sugar (or Splenda®), soy sauce, and vinegar. Chill.

Bring 4 cups of water to a rolling boil. Put the broccoli florets in a colander and pour the water slowly over them to blanch. When cool, break apart larger florets so they are all a similar size.

Combine florets with raisins or dried cranberries and oranges, if using, and enough dressing to lightly coat. Cover and refrigerate until ready to serve.

Just before serving, fold in pecans and green onions.

Chicken and Spinach Salad

Ingredients

About 2 servings

8 ounces fresh spinach
2 oranges, peeled and cut into chunks
2 cups cooked and cubed chicken
1 cup sliced strawberries

Dressing:

3 tablespoons red wine vinegar
3 teaspoons orange juice
1 1/2 tablespoons oil
1/4 teaspoon dry mustard
1 teaspoon poppy seeds

Directions

Mix dressing ingredients and refrigerate.

Wash spinach and break into bite size pieces. Add oranges, chicken, and strawberries. Serve with dressing.

Pasta Broccoli Salad

Family favorite of Joyce Spozio

Ingredients

12 cloves of garlic, chopped fine
4 cups broccoli florets
1/2 cup olive oil
12 ounces spiral pasta
Parmesan cheese

Directions

Sauté first three items together. (Do not burn garlic as it will become bitter.)

Cook 12 ounces spiral pasta according to package directions and drain.

Toss broccoli mixture and pasta together. Sprinkle with Parmesan cheese (fresh is best).

Serve hot or cold.

Grandma's Potato Salad

Ingredients

9 potatoes, peeled and cooked; dice when cooled
5 stalks celery, diced
1 large white onion, finely diced
3/4 cup pickle relish
1 tablespoon mustard
6 hard boiled eggs, cooled and diced
1 1/2 cups mayonnaise
Pepper and salt to taste
Paprika

Directions

Gently mix together. Put in bowl and sprinkle with paprika. Best if chilled overnight.

Strawberry Imperial

Ingredients

1 large package strawberry flavored gelatin

20-ounce can crushed pineapple

3 small bananas, sliced

1 small carton frozen strawberries

4 ounces (small carton) sour cream

Directions

Dissolve gelatin in 1 cup of hot water. Add partially thawed strawberries and stir until thawed. Add bananas, pineapple, and juice to mixture.

Pour half of mixture into another bowl and refrigerate until set. Spread sour cream on top of "set" mixture. Pour remaining mixture on top and refrigerate until set.

Cut into squares and serve cold.

Crepes

Ingredients

Makes 14 crepes

1 1/2 cups all-purpose flour
1 tablespoon sugar
1/2 teaspoon baking powder
1/2 teaspoon salt
2 cups milk
2 tablespoons margarine or butter, melted
2 eggs
(If making dessert crepes, add 1/2 teaspoon vanilla.)

Directions

Mix flour, sugar, baking powder, and salt in 1 1/2-quart bowl. Stir in remaining ingredients. Beat with hand beater until smooth.

Butter 6- or 8-inch skillet and heat over medium heat until bubbly. For each crepe pour 1/4 cup of batter in center of skillet. Rotate pan until thin film covers bottom. Cook until light brown. Flip and cook other side. Stack crepes with waxed paper between and cover.

These crepes freeze well. May be filled with chicken broccoli filling or spinach mushroom, or use as a dessert crepe and fill with fruit.

Chicken Broccoli Crepes

Ingredients

3 cups diced cooked chicken
2 cups chopped broccoli, steamed

Sauté:
1 cup chopped mushrooms
1/2 cup diced green onions

Sauce: 4 cups

Roux:
1/4 cup margarine and 1/4 cup flour. Mix the
  flour into the melted margarine.
1 cup chopped carrots
1/2 cup chopped onions
3 cups chicken broth
1/2 cup white wine
Pinch of nutmeg
1 bay leaf
1 cup milk
Salt and pepper to taste

Directions

Combine all the ingredients for the sauce and stir until thickened on medium heat (do not boil).

Combine the chicken, broccoli, mushrooms, and green onions and a little sauce.

Place a layer of this mixture in the center of the crepe and fold over. Place the crepe seam side down on the serving plate and spoon some sauce over the top. Be sure the crepe is covered with sauce.

Chicken and Black Bean Tostadas

Ingredients

Serves 4

2 lb broiler chicken
1 large tomato
1 small head romaine lettuce
1 green onion
1 package taco seasoning (1 1/4 ounces)
15-ounce can black beans, drained
4 flour tortillas
1 medium ripe avocado
1/3 cup sour cream or plain nonfat yogurt
Prepared Mexican salsa and fresh cilantro or
  parsley for garnish

Directions

Roast chicken in 350° oven 1 hour or until cooked through. Remove from heat and allow to cool. Discard bones and skin from chicken; shred meat and reserve.

Dice tomato, thinly slice lettuce, and dice green onion.

Preheat oven to 450°.

In 3-quart saucepan over medium heat, bring to boil shredded chicken, taco seasoning mix, and 1 cup water. Reduce heat to low and simmer 5 minutes to blend flavors, stirring occasionally. Stir in onion and beans.

Meanwhile, place flour tortillas on cookie sheet and toast in oven about 3 minutes until crisp, but not brown.

Cut avocado into slices, removing rind.

Place each toasted tortilla on plate, top with sliced lettuce, chicken mixture, diced tomato, and dollops of sour cream or yogurt. Garnish with salsa, cilantro, or parsley. Arrange lettuce leaves around outside edge of plate.

Apricot Chicken

Ingredients

One of our most popular dishes; easy to make for unexpected guests

8 chicken breasts (uniform size, pound out
  if too thick)

16 ounces apricot preserves, pureed

2 packages of dry onion soup mix

1 large bottle of Catalina dressing

Directions

Preheat over to 350°.

Put chicken pieces in greased baking dish.

Mix remaining ingredients and pour over chicken;
place in oven, covered. Bake 45–60 minutes.

Cajun Chicken

Ingredients

Marinade:

    1/4 cup Amaretto

    3/4 cup buttermilk

    1 lb boneless chicken breast, cut into bite-size pieces

    Marinate 2–8 hours

Spice Mix (in blender):

    1/2 cup flour

    2 ounces almonds

    1 teaspoon dried oregano

    2 teaspoons paprika

    2 teaspoons ground cumin

    1/8 teaspoon cayenne pepper

    1/4 teaspoon salt

    Pulse together until finely ground.

Directions

Drain chicken and toss in spice mix. Cook chicken in oil (canola or vegetable) over medium heat until golden and crispy. Drain on paper towel.

Dipping Sauce:

    2 tablespoons Amaretto

    1/3 cup honey

    1/3 cup Dijon mustard

Chicken Breast Supreme

Ingredients

4 chicken breasts, boned

6 strips lean bacon

10 1/2-ounce can condensed cream of mushroom soup

10 1/2-ounce can condensed cream of celery soup

Dry sherry (a dash)

3/4 lb dried beef

8 ounces sour cream

Sliced button mushrooms

Salt and pepper to taste

Directions

Pound out boneless chicken breasts. Lay two slices of dried beef on top of each breast. Roll breasts and fasten with toothpicks. Wrap rolls with bacon and place in baking dish.

In a bowl, mix soups, sour cream, salt, and pepper. Pour over chicken breasts.

Bake covered with foil at 300° for 2 1/2 hours or until done. Increase heat to 325° and cook 30 minutes more, basting with sauce and adding sherry. You may also add some sliced or button mushrooms for the last 30 minutes of cooking time.

Chicken Divan

Ingredients

Serves 7

7 boneless skinless chicken breasts (flatten chicken for tenderness)
Salt and pepper to taste
Oil
Fresh broccoli (3 to 4 large stems)
1 can cream of chicken soup
1 can cream of celery soup
1 cup toasted silvered almonds
3/4 to 1 cup mayonnaise
1 teaspoon curry powder (to taste—maybe a little more)
2 tablespoon fresh lemon juice
Sprinkle of black or white pepper
Sharp cheddar
1 cup homemade day old white bread crumbs
Paprika
Chopped parsley

Directions

Heat the oil. Salt and pepper the chicken and sauté until done, turning in the pan to cook evenly. Cut each breast into uneven, large pieces.

Cut off stems and cook the broccoli in boiling water for 2–3 minutes; then drain and put under cold/ice water to stop cooking.

Mix soups, almonds, mayonnaise, curry, lemon juice, and pepper. Mix chicken in a little of the above mixture, leaving a lot in the bowl. Then lay the chicken pieces in the bottom of a 9 x 14-inch pan.

Lay broccoli along the sides and top of pan around chicken. Add the remaining mixture on top of chicken but do not cover broccoli (for looks).

Sprinkle sharp cheddar cheese on top, followed by fresh bread crumbs; sprinkle with paprika.

If you make ahead, only add cheese and bread crumbs right before cooking.

Bake at 350° for 20–30 minutes until just bubbly.

Chicken and Dumplings

Ingredients

1 whole chicken, cooked (save broth)
2 cups all-purpose flour
1 teaspoon salt
Dash of pepper
1 can cream of chicken soup

Directions

After chicken cools enough to handle, remove the bones. Return chicken to broth.

Mix flour, salt, pepper, and cream of chicken soup, adding more flour to make a stiff dough. Roll out on a floured board until about as thin as pie crust. Cut into strips.

Bring chicken broth to a boil. Drop dumplings into broth one at a time. Do not stir. Reduce heat to a simmer. Cook uncovered 15 minutes. Cover and cook 15 minutes more.

Chicken Melanaise

Ingredients

6 chicken breasts
1/2 teaspoon white pepper
2 cups milk
1 1/2 cups Italian seasoned bread crumbs
1 teaspoon seasoned salt
4 eggs
1 1/2 cups flour

Directions

Mix seasoned salt, white pepper, and flour together in a bowl.

Mix eggs and milk together in a bowl.

Dip each chicken breast in flour mixture, then in egg mixture, and then in bread crumbs.

Bake chicken breasts on greased baking sheet at 350° for 45 minutes.

Mexican Chicken

Ingredients

1/2 cup diced onion

1/2 cup diced celery

1/2 cup diced bell pepper

1 cup chicken broth

10 3/4-ounce can cream of mushroom soup

10 3/4-ounce can cream of chicken soup

10-ounce can tomatoes and green chilies

1 teaspoon chili powder

1 teaspoon garlic powder

4 cups diced cooked chicken

12 corn tortillas

2 cups shredded cheddar cheese

Directions

Sauté onion, celery, and bell pepper. Blend soups, 1/2 cup broth, chili powder, and garlic powder until smooth. Combine sautéed vegetables and soup mixture. Add tomatoes and green chilies and chicken.

Preheat oven to 350°. Lightly mist 9 x 13 casserole dish with nonstick cooking spray.

Begin forming layers in casserole dish by dipping tortillas in remaining broth and covering bottom of dish. Cover with soup mixture and repeat layers. Top with grated cheese.

Bake 1 hour, uncovered.

Chicken with Mushrooms and Artichokes

Ingredients

Chicken:
6 chicken breasts, flattened
1/2 cup flour
Salt and black pepper
1 teaspoon chopped garlic
1/2 cup chopped green onion

Sauce:
2 cups chicken broth
1 cup white wine
1 cup half-and-half
2 cups quartered mushrooms
2 cups quartered artichoke hearts
1 tablespoon fresh chopped parsley
1/4 teaspoon butter
1/4 teaspoon flour
Salt and pepper to taste

Directions

Dip chicken in flour (season with salt and pepper). Sauté in margarine or butter.

Make roux with 1/4 teaspoon butter and 1/4 teaspoon flour. (Simply mix the room temperature butter and the flour in a small bowl or cup.) Add roux to garlic and green onion and then add broth wine, half-and-half, mushrooms, artichoke hearts, parsley, and salt and pepper. Heat and pour sauce over sautéed chicken.

After you sauté chicken, remove it. Add 1 teaspoon chopped garlic, 1/2 cup chopped green onion. Pour the sauce over the sautéed chicken and enjoy.

Parmesan Chicken

Ingredients

6 chicken breasts
3 eggs, beaten
2 cups Parmesan cheese
2 cups bread crumbs
Salt and pepper to taste

Directions

Dip chicken into beaten eggs and then into dry mixture.

Place chicken breasts on a prepared cookie sheet sprayed with nonstick vegetable oil—or use baking sheets. Bake at 350° for 20–30 minutes until golden brown.

Pecan Chicken with Roasted Red Bell Pepper Sauce

Ingredients

8 boneless chicken breasts, flattened

6 eggs, beaten

Seasoned salt and pepper to taste

1 lb butter

2 cups milk

3 cups flour

3 cups chopped pecans

3 cups bread crumbs

Roasted Red Bell Pepper Sauce:

3 sliced red bell peppers

3 chopped shallots

1/2 lb butter

1/2 cup white wine

1 1/2 quarts whipping cream

1 large can chicken broth

Directions

For chicken, mix beaten eggs and milk in a bowl. Mix flour and seasonings. Mix pecans and bread crumbs.

Dip chicken in flour, then egg and milk, and then roll in pecans and bread crumbs. Sauté chicken in butter on each side until lightly browned.

Place chicken in baking dish and bake at 350° for 35–45 minutes or until done.

For Roasted Red Bell Pepper Sauce, sauté shallots and red bell peppers in butter. Add chicken broth and wine. Simmer for 10 minutes. Add cream, stirring once or twice. Cook until tender. Puree in food processor. Strain and serve over chicken.

Chicken-Rice Supper

Ingredients

Serving 6

1/4 cup margarine or butter
1/3 cup all-purpose flour
1 1/3 teaspoon salt
1/8 teaspoon pepper
1 1/2 cups milk
1 cup chicken broth
2 cut up cooked chicken or turkey
1 1/2 cups cooked white rice or wild rice
1/3 cup chopped green pepper
1/3 cup silvered almonds
2 tablespoons chopped pimento
1 4-ounce can mushrooms, drained
Parsley for garnish

Directions

Heat margarine in 2-quart saucepan until melted. Stir in flour, salt, and pepper. Cook, stirring constantly until bubbly; remove from heat. Stir in milk and broth. Heat to boiling, stirring constantly for 1 minute. Stir in remaining ingredients.

Pour into an ungreased 2-quart casserole or rectangular baking dish (10 x 8 x 1 1/2-inch). Bake uncovered at 350° until bubbly (about 40–45 minutes). Garnish with parsley if desired.

Rosemary Chicken

Ingredients

6 chicken breasts or half of a chicken
1/4 cup diced fresh rosemary
2 tablespoons Dijon mustard
1/2 cup chopped green onion
1/4 cup lemon juice
1/2 cup salad oil
1/2 cup olive oil
4 cloves chopped garlic
Dash of black pepper and salt

Directions

Marinate chicken overnight in all ingredients
The marinated chicken breasts may be grilled or panfried.

Chicken Spaghetti

Ingredients

Serves 8

4 cups cubed cooked chicken
Cooked spaghetti (cooked in chicken broth)
1 cup chopped sautéed onions
1 cup chopped bell pepper

Sauce:

10 3/4-ounce can cream of chicken soup
1 lb cubed Velveeta® cheese
10-ounce can Rotel® tomatoes
1 tablespoon Worcestershire sauce
1 cup sliced mushrooms
Salt and pepper to taste

Directions

Combine the sauce ingredients in a saucepan, and stir together until the cheese melts.

Combine all ingredients and place in a casserole dish. Bake 30 minutes at 325°, until bubbly.

Chicken Tarragon

Ingredients

4 chicken breasts, cut into pieces

1/4 cup of flour

3/4 cup butter

Dash salt

1 tablespoon dried tarragon

2 cups chicken broth

1/4 cup Dijon mustard

2 tablespoons dry parsley

2 cups of cooked white rice

2 lemons thinly sliced, seeds removed

Directions

Sauté chicken in 1/2 cup butter.

Make a roux of 1/4 cup of the butter and 1/4 cup flour (mix room temperature butter with the flour).

Mix the ingredients for the sauce over medium heat until thickened. Add chicken and juices into mixture and add lemon slices.

Serve with white rice.

Chicken Tetrazzini

Ingredients

10-ounce package white noodles

6-ounce package spinach noodles

1 small can water chestnuts, sliced

14-ounce jar diced pimentos

3 small green onions, diced

2-ounce can sliced black olives

4 cups diced cooked chicken

Sauce:

Roux of margarine and flour (mix together 4 tablespoons of margarine and 1/2 cup of flour in a cup)

14 ounces chicken broth

3 cups milk

Black or white pepper to taste

1/2 cup sherry wine

2 tablespoons lemon juice

1 1/2 teaspoons garlic powder

1/2 teaspoon onion powder

2 tablespoons Parmesan cheese

1 lb Velveeta® cheese, cubed

Directions

Mix all ingredients for the sauce over medium heat until cheese is melted. Add chestnuts, pimentos, green onions, black olives, and chicken to sauce; it will be thin but will soak into the noodles.

Boil the noodles in boiling salted water until tender yet firm.

After combining the noodles and sauce, place in a casserole dish and bake at 325° until bubbly.

Crustless Crab Quiche

Recipe from Shirley Hoppe

Ingredients

1/2 lb crab
2 tablespoons butter
1/2 lb mushrooms
4 eggs
1 cup small curd cottage cheese
1 cup grated Parmesan cheese
1/4 cup flour
1 teaspoon onion flakes
1/4 teaspoon salt
6 drops Tabasco® sauce
2 cups grated Monterey Jack cheese
Parsley

Directions

Sauté crab and mushrooms in butter. In a separate bowl, blend together 4 eggs, cottage cheese, Parmesan cheese, flour, onion flakes, salt, Tabasco® sauce, and 1 1/2 cups grated cheese. Add crab and mushrooms.

Spray glass 9 x 5 x 13-inch casserole dish with vegetable spray. Pour mixture into casserole. Top with 1/2 cup grated cheese and a sprinkle of parsley.

Bake 350° for 40 minutes.

Crawfish Etoufee

Ingredients

1 stick margarine
1 lb crawfish tails (or shrimp), peeled
1 medium onion, chopped
2 ribs celery, chopped
1/2 bell pepper, chopped
1 tablespoon paprika
1/2 teaspoon salt
1/4 teaspoon black pepper
2 cups chicken broth
1 tablespoon parsley, chopped
1 tablespoon green onion tops, cut with scissors
Cooked rice

Directions

Bring water to boil in large pot (do not use a black iron pot). Add crawfish tails and cook for 2–3 minutes. Remove crawfish tails with slotted spoon and set aside. Discard water.

Melt margarine and add onion, celery, bell pepper, and seasonings. Sauté for 10 minutes. Return crawfish tails to pan and add chicken broth. Stir and cook slowly, covered, for about 40 minutes.

Serve over hot rice and sprinkle with parsley and green onion tops.

Eggplant Parmesan

Ingredients

1 medium eggplant (about 1 1/2 lbs)
1 teaspoon salt
1/4 cup margarine or butter, melted
2 eggs
1 cup dry bread crumbs
1/4 cup Parmesan cheese
1/2 teaspoon dried basil leaves
1/2 teaspoon parsley flakes
3 cups marinara
16 ounces mozzarella cheese

Directions

Just before cooking, wash eggplant and, if desired, remove skin. Cut into 1/2-inch slices.

Sprinkle cut sides with salt. Let drain in colander 30 minutes; blot with paper towel.

Beat margarine and eggs. Mix remaining ingredients. Dip eggplant slices into egg mixture, then into bread crumb mixture. Either place in skillet with butter and brown (be sure to drain well) or place on greased broiler pan and broil in oven about 5 inches from heat, turning once, until light golden brown, about 4 minutes (again, be sure to drain well).

Place in prepared casserole dish in layers with marinara sauce and mozzarella cheese. Bake at 350° for about 40 minutes, covered. Sprinkle with more mozzarella cheese and brown about 5 minutes more.

Osso Buco
(Veal Shank)

Ingredients

2 Provomi veal shanks

Seasoning salt

Extra virgin olive oil

Rosemary

Fresh ground pepper

2 cups Chianti wine

2 teaspoons margarine

6 ounces Chianti wine

1/2 sliced onion

4 bouillon cubes

14 ounces water

1 cup tomato paste

1 cup flour

1 cup peas

1/2 cup Italian parsley

Directions

Season veal shanks lightly on both sides with seasoning salt. Coat lightly with flour. Sauté both sides with extra virgin olive oil until brown. Add a pinch of rosemary, and pepper lightly. Add 2 cups Chianti wine and margarine. Cover and let sauté for 30 minutes, turning shanks two times. Add 6 more ounces Chianti wine and onion.

Prepare bouillon cubes in 14 ounces water; add to veal shank. Add tomato paste; mix and stir. Bake in 325° oven for 2 hours.

Garnish with peas and Italian parsley.

Bacon Popovers

Ingredients

Makes 6 popovers

3 slices bacon or 3 tablespoons grated
  Parmesan cheese
1 tablespoon shortening
2 eggs, beaten
1 cup milk
1 tablespoon cooking oil or bacon drippings
1 cup all-purpose flour

Directions

If using bacon, cook bacon until crisp; drain, reserving 1 tablespoon drippings if desired. Finely crumble bacon. Set aside.

Using 1/2 teaspoon shortening for each cup, grease the bottom and sides of six cups of a popover pan. (Or, use six 6-ounce custard cups. Place greased custard cups in a 15 x 10 x 1-inch baking pan.) Set aside.

In a mixing bowl, combine eggs, milk, and oil (or bacon drippings). Add flour and bacon or grated Parmesan. Beat with a rotary beater or wire whisk until mixture is smooth. Fill the prepared cups half full. Bake in a 400° oven about 40 minutes, or until very firm.

Immediately remove popovers from the oven and prick each with a fork to let steam escape. (If crisper popovers are desired, after baking, prick the popovers, turn off the oven and leave popovers in the oven for 5–10 minutes more.) Serve hot.

Cheesy Grits

Ingredients

2 cups milk

2 cups water

1 teaspoon salt

1/2 teaspoon pepper

1 cup white hominy quick grits

1 1/2 sliced green onions, with tops

2 eggs, slightly beaten

1 tablespoon margarine or butter

1/4 teaspoon paprika

1 cup grated cheddar cheese

Directions

Heat milk, water, salt, and pepper to boiling in a 2-quart saucepan. Gradually add grits, stirring constantly; reduce heat. Add cheese, margarine, paprika, and onions. Stir 1 cup of hot mix into the eggs, then add the remaining hot mix.

Rice Dressing

Ingredients

16 ounce package of Uncle Ben's Long Grain &
  Wild Rice Original, cooked according to box
1/2 cup chopped green onion
1 cup chopped sweet onion
1 cup chopped celery
1 cup chopped bell pepper
1/2 stick butter
1 cup sliced water chestnuts
2 cups sliced fresh mushrooms
1 1/2 cups chicken broth
1 can (10 3/4 ounces) cream of chicken soup
1 can (10 3/4 ounces) cream of mushroom soup
2 eggs, beaten
1 cup sliced almonds

Directions

Sauté green onions, sweet onions, celery, and bell pepper in 1/2 stick butter. Add water chestnuts, mushrooms, chicken broth, and cans of soup.

Add the mixed ingredients to rice with 2 beaten eggs. Pour into greased casserole dish and top with sliced almonds. Bake 350° for 1 hour.

Egg Brunch Casserole

Ingredients

2 cups seasoned croutons

1 cup shredded cheddar cheese

4 eggs

2 cups milk

1/2 teaspoon prepared mustard

1/4 teaspoon onion powder

6 slices bacon, crisply fried

Salt and pepper to taste

Directions

Mix croutons and cheese in bottom of long, flat casserole dish. Beat eggs in mixing bowl and add milk, mustard, onion powder, and seasonings. Pour egg mixture over croutons and cheese. Crumble bacon on top of casserole. Bake at 325° for about 55–60 minutes.

Strata

Ingredients

15 eggs, beaten
15 slices of bread, torn into small pieces
2 cups milk
2 cups shredded cheddar cheese or shredded jalapeño cheese
Salt and pepper to taste

Directions

Place 15 slices of torn bread in 9 x 11-inch baking dish.

Add 2 cups milk to 15 slices of bread. Mix eggs, salt and pepper, and 1 cup cheese; and pour mixture over bread and milk. Add one cup of cheese on the top.

Bake at 350° for 30–45 minutes, or until it puffs and browns on top.

Ham and Cheese Fritters

Ingredients

Makes about 30 fritters

1 1/2 cups flour
1 tablespoon Dijon mustard
1 1/2 cups (1/4 inch cubes) cooked ham
1/2 cup cubed cheddar cheese
2 teaspoons baking powder
1/2 teaspoon salt
2/3 cup milk
2 eggs, separated
1 tablespoon oil, plus some extra for frying

Directions

In a large bowl, combine flour, baking powder, and salt. Combine milk, egg yolks, oil, and mustard; stir into flour mixture until combined. Fold in ham and cheese. Beat egg whites until stiff; fold into batter.

In heavy pot, heat 3 inches oil over medium heat until very hot but not smoking. Using two spoons, carefully add batter, one tablespoon at a time, to oil.

Cook fritters until just starting to turn golden grown along edges, about 60–90 seconds. Using slotted spoon, turn fritters; cook until golden and cooked through, 60–90 seconds or more. Remove with slotted spoon; drain on paper towels.

Italian Cheese Sticks

Ingredients

1 cup flour

2 tablespoons freshly grated Parmesan cheese

1/2 teaspoon garlic powder

1/4 teaspoon dried basil

1/4 teaspoon dried oregano

1/4 teaspoon dried rosemary

1/4 teaspoon salt

1/4 teaspoon onion powder

1/2 cup cold butter cut into small pats

1 cup shredded sharp cheddar cheese

3 tablespoons cold water

Directions

Preheat oven to 425°.

In a large bowl, mix together flour, Parmesan cheese, garlic powder, onion powder, basil, oregano, rosemary, and salt. Using a pastry blender, cut cold butter into flour mixture until it resembles coarse meal. Add cheddar cheese and mix until well blended. Add water (1 tablespoon at a time), mixing well after each addition.

Roll portions of dough and cut into 1/2-inch strips. Place on greased baking sheet and bake 12–15 minutes.

White Sauce

Ingredients

2 tablespoons margarine or butter
2 tablespoons flour
1/4 teaspoon salt
1/8 teaspoon pepper
1 cup milk

Directions

Heat margarine or butter in 1 1/2 quart saucepan over low heat until melted. Stir in flour, salt, and pepper and cook over low heat, stirring constantly until smooth and bubbly. Stir in milk and heat to boiling. Continue stirring for 1 minute.

Variations:

Add 1/2 teaspoon curry powder.

Stir in 1/4 teaspoon dry mustard. Add 1/2 cup cheddar or Swiss cheese and stir until melted.

Corn Soufflé

Ingredients

1 cup cream-style corn

1 cup whole kernel corn

1 small box corn muffin mix

1 cup sour cream

3 eggs

1 stick melted margarine

1/4 cup mayonnaise

1 cup grated cheddar cheese

Directions

Grease a 2-quart casserole dish. Slightly beat 3 eggs and mix in rest of ingredients, except cheese. Add mixture to dish.

Bake at 350° for 40–45 minutes, until knife inserted in the middle comes out clean.

Take out of oven, sprinkle cheese on top, and put back in oven until cheese melts (about 5 minutes).

Carrot Orzo

Recipe from Barbara Echols

Ingredients

1 cup baby carrots, chopped

2 tablespoons butter

1 cup orzo

1 cup water

1 cup chicken broth

1 clove garlic, chopped

1 cup grated Parmesan cheese

2 tablespoons chopped green onion

1 teaspoon minced rosemary sprigs

Salt and pepper

Directions

Finely chop carrots in a food processor.

Melt butter in saucepan. Add orzo and carrots. Sauté until orzo is golden (about 5 minutes). Add water, broth, and garlic and cook uncovered over medium heat until all liquid is absorbed (stir frequently). Stir in cheese, onion, rosemary, salt, and pepper to taste.

Squash Casserole

Ingredients

2 cups sliced yellow squash

1 10 3/4-ounce can cream of chicken soup

1 cup shredded carrots

1/2 cup butter

1/2 teaspoon white pepper

1/2 cup onion, chopped in large pieces

8 ounces sour cream

1 8-ounce package herb stuffing mix

1 teaspoon salt

Directions

Cook squash and onion in boiling salt water for 5 minutes until tender. Drain.

In a bowl, combine soup, shredded carrots, salt and pepper, and sour cream. Fold in well-drained squash and onion.

Melt butter in skillet. Add stuffing mix and stir until coated.

In the bottom of a 9 x 13-inch baking dish, put half of the stuffing crumbs. Pour in squash mixture. Spread remaining crumbs on top. Bake at 350° for 30–40 minutes.

Polenta Casserole

Ingredients

Serves 8

Tomato Mixture :

    1/2 cup sun-dried tomatoes

    2 zucchini, thinly sliced lengthwise

    1 red onion, sliced 1/4 inch thick

    Olive oil for brushing

    1 teaspoon olive oil

    5 cloves garlic, minced

    2 teaspoons fresh rosemary leaves, chopped

    1/2 cup black olives

    Salt and pepper to taste

Polenta:

    3 ounces goat cheese, crumbled

    2 1/2 cups polenta

    2 tablespoons butter or margarine

    1/2 cup grated Parmesan cheese (optional)

    Salt to taste

Directions

Soak sun-dried tomatoes in hot water for 30 minutes; drain and chop. Brush zucchini and onion with olive oil; grill or broil until charred and soft. Set aside zucchini and chopped onion.

Heat oil in a small sauté pan over medium-low heat. Sauté garlic until fragrant. Add onion, rosemary, olives, tomatoes, salt, and pepper; set aside.

Bring 5 cups lightly salted water to a boil. Drizzle in polenta, stirring constantly with a wooden spoon. Cook polenta 20 minutes, stirring often. Add butter if desired. Add cheese and salt, stirring until ingredients are incorporated and polenta is thick and creamy.

Preheat oven to 350°.

Brush inside of a 9 x 10-inch shallow baking dish with olive oil. Pour half of the polenta into dish; smooth surface to level. Arrange zucchini slices over polenta; top with onion mixture.

Sprinkle goat cheese over onion mixture. Pour remaining polenta on top; smooth. Sprinkle with Parmesan cheese. Bake 20–30 minutes or until warmed through. Cool 5 minutes before serving.

Sweet Potato Casserole
Kim's Recipe

Ingredients

Serves 6 people

3 cups mashed sweet potatoes
1 cup evaporated milk
1 cup sugar
1 stick butter, melted
2 beaten eggs
2 teaspoons vanilla

Topping:
1 cup brown sugar
1/3 cup flour
1/4 cup melted butter
1/2 cup chopped pecans

Directions

Mix sweet potatoes, evaporated milk, sugar, butter, eggs, and vanilla. Pour in a buttered pan. Mix topping ingredients and put on top of potato mixture. Bake at 350° for 20–30 minutes.

Wine Mushroom Chicken

Recipe from Larry Wilkes

Ingredients

Serves 4

4 chicken breasts (8 ounces each)
1/2 stick butter
1 cup chopped green onions or shallots
5 large cloves of garlic, minced
1/2 cup white wine
2 cups whipping cream
2 cups sliced mushrooms
1 cup flour
Salt and white pepper to taste
Cooked rice

Directions

Pound out chicken if too thick. Dip in flour, salt, and white pepper.

Sauté chicken in butter until cooked. Remove chicken. Add onions, garlic, wine, and whipping cream. Bring to boil, stirring constantly. Add mushrooms and cooked chicken to pan for 5 minutes.

Serve over rice.

Desserts

Amaretto Brownies

Ingredients

3/4 lb (3 sticks) butter
3/4 lb (12 ounces) chocolate chips
8 eggs
3 cups sugar
2 cups flour
1/4 tablespoon salt
2 1/2 cups pecans
1/2 cup Amaretto

Directions

Melt butter and chocolate chips in a medium saucepan. Put in mixing bowl to cool. Add eggs, sugar, flour, salt, and pecans.

Bake at 350° in a sprayed 9 x 13-inch pan for about 60 minutes or until a toothpick inserted 2 inches from side of pan comes out almost clean.

When cool, poke holes with toothpicks in top. Brush with Amaretto. Spread with chocolate frosting if desired.

Bread Pudding

Ingredients

3 cups milk

2/3 cup raisins

1 cup sugar

1 teaspoon cinnamon

1/4 teaspoon allspice

1 (24 inch) loaf day-old French bread,
  cut into 1 1/2-inch cubes

1 16-ounce can fancy fruit cocktail,
  drained, cherries removed

1 29-ounce can peach halves, drained,
  cut into large chunks

1/2 cup melted butter

1 teaspoon vanilla

1/2 teaspoon nutmeg

1/2 teaspoon salt

Directions

Scald milk in large saucepan. Remove from heat and allow to cool for 5 minutes; add bread, fruit cocktail, peaches, raisins, and melted butter and mix thoroughly.

In a separate bowl, beat the eggs and add sugar, vanilla, cinnamon, nutmeg, allspice, and salt. Mix until blended; add to bread mixture. Blend well.

Butter a 3-quart glass casserole on all inner surfaces. Pour in mixture and distribute evenly. Bake uncovered at 350° for 70 minutes, or until a knife comes out clean and top begins to brown and form a crust.

Allow to cool at room temperature.

Brandy Sauce for Bread Pudding

Ingredients

3 eggs
1/4 cup sugar
1/2 teaspoon vanilla
4 tablespoons butter, melted
1/4 cup brandy
1/8 teaspoon ground cloves
1/2 cup milk

Directions

In a heavy 3-quart saucepan, beat eggs thoroughly. Add sugar, vanilla, and butter; heat slowly, stirring constantly, until mixture begins to thicken. Remove from heat and add brandy, cloves, and milk, stirring constantly. When well-mixed, place sauce in blender and beat at high speed for 1 1/2 minutes, or until sauce has texture of very heavy cream. Serve over bread pudding.

Chocolate Sheet Cake

Ingredients

Easy to make and delicious!

2 cups sugar
2 cups flour
1/2 cup cocoa
1 teaspoon baking soda
1/2 teaspoon salt
1 cup butter or margarine
1 cup water
1/2 cup buttermilk
2 eggs
1 teaspoon vanilla

Frosting:

1/2 cup butter or margarine
1/4 cup cocoa
6 tablespoons milk (1/8 cup)
4 cups powdered sugar
1 cup chopped walnuts or pecans

Directions

Combine sugar, flour, cocoa, baking soda, and salt and mix well. Heat butter and water until boiling; pour over dry ingredients. Beat in buttermilk, eggs, and vanilla. Pour thin batter into greased, floured 9 x 13-inch pan.

Bake at 400° for about 30 minutes, or until toothpick inserted in center comes out clean.

While cake is cooking, combine butter, cocoa, and milk and heat to boiling—this will be thick. Pour over sugar and nuts and mix well. Allow cake to cool for 5 minutes and spread frosting gently over warm cake. Frosting will melt and spread over cake.

Chocolate Nut Slices

Ingredients

1 cup sugar

1 cup packed brown sugar

2/3 cup shortening

2/3 cup margarine or butter

2 eggs

3 1/4 cups all-purpose flour

1 cup finely chopped nuts

1/2 cup cocoa

1 teaspoon soda

1 teaspoon salt

Directions

Mix sugar, brown sugar, shortening, buter, and eggs well.

Stir flour, nuts, cocoa, baking soda, and salt into butter mixture.

Divide and make 3-inch diameter rolls. Refrigerate 2 hours. Preheat oven to 350°. Slice 1/4 inch (or thinner), and bake 9–12 minutes. Dip in chocolate.

For butterscotch, omit the cocoa powder.

Egg Nog Pound Cake

Ingredients

1 (18–25 ounce) package yellow cake mix

1 (4 serving size) package instant vanilla pudding
 and pie filling mix

1/2 cup egg nog

3/4 cup vegetable oil

4 eggs

1/2 teaspoon ground nutmeg

Powdered sugar, if desired

Directions

Preheat oven to 350°.

In large mixing bowl combine cake mix, pudding mix, egg nog, and oil; beat at low speed with electric mixer until moistened. Add eggs and nutmeg; beat at medium-high speed for 4 minutes.

Pour into greased and floured 10-inch fluted or tube pan. Bake 40–45 minutes or until toothpick inserted near center comes out clean.

Cool 10 minutes; remove from pan. Cool completely. Sprinkle with powdered sugar if desired.

Apple Cake

Ingredients

Makes 2 9-inch bundt pans

3 cups sugar

2 cups oil

6 eggs

4 cups flour

3 teaspoons cinnamon

2 teaspoons soda

2 teaspoons vanilla

1 teaspoon salt

1/2 teaspoon nutmeg

6 cups chopped apples (can use peeled and
cored fresh apples or canned apples)

2 cups chopped nuts

Directions

Mix all ingredients in order and pour equally into nonstick bundt pans. Bake at 350° for 1 hour.

Coconut Cream Cake

Ingredients

Serves 12

This cake takes a little work, but it is worth it. My first time to bake this cake was Mother's Day, and it was eaten to the last crumb with rave reviews.

1 15-ounce can unsweetened coconut milk

5 teaspoons cornstarch

1/2 cup half-and-half

1/4 cup plus 1/4 cup granulated sugar

Pinch of salt

4 large egg yolks

1/2 teaspoon pure vanilla extract

1 teaspoon unsalted butter

1/2 cup toasted coconut, finely shredded

3 1/2 cups all-purpose flour

2 1/2 teaspoons baking powder

2 1/2 teaspoons baking soda

1/2 teaspoon salt

1 lb. unsalted butter, softened

2 1/2 cups granulated sugar

7 large egg yolks

1 tablespoon pure vanilla extract

1 3/4 cups milk

7 large egg whites

1/4 teaspoon cream of tartar

4 ounces butter, room temperature

4 ounces cream cheese, room temperature

3 cups confectioners' sugar

3 tablespoons whipping cream

2 tablespoons pure vanilla extract

Pinch of salt

1 cup coconut to finish, finely shredded

Directions

To prepare the filling, mix 3 tablespoons of the coconut milk with the cornstarch. Set aside.

In a medium-sized saucepan, bring the remaining coconut milk, half-and-half, 1/4 cup sugar, and salt to a simmer over medium-high heat, stirring for 2 minutes or until sugar is dissolved.

Whisk together 4 egg yolks, 1/4 cup sugar and 1/2 teaspoon vanilla in a medium bowl. Slowly pour in the coconut milk mixture, whisking continuously.

Return the liquid to the saucepan; whisk continuously while the cream simmers over low heat until it begins to thicken (about 5 minutes).

Whisk in the cornstarch mixture, cook for 2 minutes and add 1 teaspoon butter. Stir until melted. Remove from heat and blend in 1/2 cup toasted coconut.

Transfer to a bowl and lay a piece of plastic wrap on top of the cream filling to prevent a skin from accumulating on the surface. Refrigerate for at least 2 hours, or until set.

Preheat oven to 350°. Butter and flour three 10-inch cake pans.

For the cake, sift the flour, baking powder, baking soda, and salt together and set aside.

In a large bowl, beat 1 lb butter on medium speed for 1 minute. Add 2 1/2 cups sugar and 7 egg yolks one at a time, beating after each addition. Add 1 tablespoon vanilla and beat until mixture is fluffy (about 3 minutes). Lower the speed and mix in half the dry ingredients. Add the milk, then the remaining dry ingredients. In a separate bowl, whip the 7 egg whites with the cream of tartar until soft peaks form. Fold some of the whites into the cake batter to loosen up the batter and prevent the whites from breaking down. Add the remaining whites, folding in gently until incorporated.

Divide batter among the three prepared pans and bake for 20 minutes or until a toothpick comes out clean when stuck in the center.

To assemble the cake, place one layer on a plate and spread with half of the coconut cream filling. Place a second layer on top of the filling and spread with the remaining filling. Place the third layer on top.

To make the frosting, beat together 4 ounces butter and cream cheese in the bowl of an electric mixer until smooth. On low speed, add the confectioners' sugar, heavy whipping cream, 2 teaspoons vanilla, and pinch of salt and beat for 1 minute. Increase the speed to high and beat until frosting becomes fluffy (about 2 minutes). Immediately spread the frosting on the cake and sprinkle with finely shredded coconut.

Rum Cake

Ingredients

1 cup butter

2 cups white sugar

4 eggs

1 cup buttermilk

1 teaspoon vanilla extract

3 cups all-purpose flour

1/2 teaspoon baking powder

1/2 teaspoon baking soda

1 pinch salt

1 teaspoon rum flavored extract

Butter Rum Glaze:

1 cup butter

1 cup white sugar

1/2 cup rum

Directions

Preheat oven to 350°. Grease and flour one 10-inch bundt pan.

Cream the butter and white sugar together. Add eggs one at a time, mixing well after each one.

Sift the flour, baking powder, baking soda, and salt together and add alternately with the buttermilk to the egg mixture. Stir in the vanilla and rum extracts. Pour batter into the prepared pan.

Bake at 350° for 1 hour.

For the glaze, melt the butter and white sugar over low heat. Remove from heat and stir in rum.

Remove cake from oven and pour all of the glaze over cake while still warm. Leave cake in pan for 2 hours before moving to serving dish.

Sour Cream Coffee Cake

Ingredients

1 1/2 cups sugar

3/4 cup margarine or butter, softened

1 1/2 teaspoons vanilla

3 eggs

3 cups all-purpose flour (If using self-rising flour, omit baking powder, baking soda, and salt.)

1 1/2 teaspoons baking powder

1 1/2 teaspoons baking soda

3/4 teaspoon salt

1 1/2 cups sour cream

Brown Sugar Filling:

1/2 cup brown sugar

1/2 cup finely chopped nuts

1 1/2 teaspoons ground cinnamon

Glaze:

1/2 cup powdered sugar

1/4 teaspoon vanilla

1–2 teaspoons milk

Beat until smooth.

Directions

Preheat oven to 325°.

Beat sugar, margariner, eggs, and vanilla in 2 1/2 quart bowl at medium speed for 2 minutes, scraping bowl occasionally. Beat in flour, baking powder, baking soda, and salt alternately with sour cream on low speed.

Spread 1/3 batter in greased tube pan, 10 x 14-inch pan or 12-cup bundt pan. Spread over that 1/3 of the filling. Repeat two times; filling will be on top. Bake 1 hour or until toothpick comes out clean.

Cool 20 minutes. Remove from pan and drizzle with glaze.

Buttermilk Chess Pie

Ingredients

1 2/3 cups granulated sugar

2/3 cup butter or margarine, melted

1/2 cup all-purpose flour

4 large eggs

1 1/2 cups buttermilk

1/2 teaspoon vanilla

Dash of salt

1 unbaked 9-inch deep-dish pie shell

Directions

Heat oven to 375°.

In large bowl combine sugar, butter, and flour. Mix well. Add eggs, one at a time, mixing well after each addition. Add buttermilk, vanilla, and salt. Mix just until blended. Do not overmix. Pour into pie shell.

Bake 45–50 minutes or until tooth pick inserted in center comes out almost clean. Do not overbake.

Pecan Pie

Ingredients

1 cup dark corn syrup
1 cup light brown sugar
1/3 teaspoon salt
1/3 cup melted butter
1 teaspoon vanilla
3 eggs well beaten
2 cups chopped roasted pecans
1 unbaked 9 inch deep dish pie shell

Directions

Cover bottom of pie shell with pecans. Mix butter and brown sugar, add syrup salt, vanilla, eggs and mix well. Pour into pie shell.

Bake pie at 350° for 60 minutes or until filling is firm.

Pecan Bars

Ingredients

Crust:
1 1/2 cups flour
1/2 cup powdered sugar
1/2 cup chilled, unsalted butter

Directions

Mix all ingredients until they reach the consistency of rice.

Press into pan and bake until golden brown. Put pecans on crust; then pour the filling from the Pecan Pie recipe over crust. Bake at 350° for 20 minutes.

Orange Glaze for Fruit

Ingredients

1/2 cup orange juice
1/4 cup water
2 tablespoons sugar
1 tablespoon cornstarch

Directions

Mix in saucepan. Heat to boiling and simmer for 1 minute. Cool.

Pour glaze on fruit and refrigerate for 1 hour.

Cream Cheese Pastry for Tarts

Ingredients

Makes 40 tarts

3 cups flour
1 teaspoon salt
3/4 lb butter
9 ounces cream cheese

Directions

Combine all ingredients. Roll into 1/8-inch thickness. Cut into 3-inch rounds. Carefully press into small muffin cups. Bake at 325° for 10 minutes.

To make pecan tarts, do not bake tarts first. Instead, place finely chopped pecans in bottom of shell and fill with pecan pie filling (page 93). Then bake at 350° for 15 minutes.

Cornbread Muffins

Ingredients

4 eggs

2 cups milk

3 cups yellow corn meal

2 cups flour

2 cups sugar

4 1/2 teaspoons baking powder

1 1/2 teaspoons salt

Directions

Mix all ingredients together. Pour into greased muffin tins and bake at 350° for about 15 minutes.

Blueberry Muffins

Ingredients

Makes 12 medium muffins or 24 mini-muffins

2 cups milk

1 cup oil

4 eggs

6 cups flour

2 cups sugar

8 teaspoons baking powder

2 teaspoons salt

4 cups well drained fresh blueberries

Directions

Preheat oven to 350°.

Stir milk and oil into eggs. Sift together and add dry ingredients. Fold in blueberries. Bake 18–20 minutes.

Banana Nut Muffins

Ingredients

1 1/2 cups all-purpose flour
1 cup chopped walnuts
1/2 cup toasted wheat germ
1/2 cup brown sugar
1 tablespoon baking powder
1 teaspoon cinnamon
1/2 teaspoon salt
1/4 teaspoon ground nutmeg
2 ripe bananas, mashed
3/4 cup milk
5 tablespoons melted butter
1 egg
Cinnamon sugar (optional)

Directions

Preheat oven to 400°. Fit twelve muffin cups with paper liners. Coat each with cooking spray.

Mix flour, walnuts, wheat germ, brown sugar, baking powder, cinnamon, salt, and nutmeg in large bowl. Stir in bananas, milk, butter, and egg. Mix just until blended.

Using an ice cream scoop, fill muffin cups evenly with batter. Sprinkle with cinnamon sugar if desired.

Bake muffins until a toothpick inserted into centers comes out clean, about 20–25 minutes. Cool 1 minute; remove from the muffin pan and cool on a wire rack.

Lemon Blossoms

Ingredients

1 8 1/2-ounce package yellow cake mix
2 1/2-ounce packages instant lemon pudding mix
4 large eggs
3/4 cup vegetable oil

Glaze:

4 cups confectioners' sugar
1/3 cup fresh lemon juice
1 lemon, zested
3 tablespoons vegetable oil
3 tablespoons water

Directions

Preheat oven to 350°.

Spray miniature muffin tins with cooking spay. Combine the cake mix, pudding mix, eggs, and oil and blend well until smooth, about 2 minutes. Pour a small amount of batter, filling muffin tin half way. Bake for 23 minutes. Turn out onto a tea towel.

To make glaze, sift the sugar into a mixing bowl. Add the lemon juice, zest, oil, and 3 tablespoons water. Mix with spoon until smooth.

With fingers, dip the cupcakes into the glaze while they are still warm, covering as much of the cake as possible. Alternately, spoon the glaze over the warm cupcakes, turning them completely to coat. Place on wire racks with waxed paper underneath to catch any drips. Let the glaze set thoroughly, about 1 hour, before storing in containers with tight-fitting lids.

Peanut Butter Kiss Cookies

Ingredients

Makes 6 dozen

1 cup butter

2/3 cup creamy peanut butter

1 cup sugar

1 cup brown sugar

2 eggs

2 teaspoons vanilla

2 2/3 cups flour

2 teaspoons baking soda

1 teaspoons salt

16 ounce package of Hershey® chocolate
  KISS candies

Directions

Blend butter, peanut butter, sugar, and brown sugar until creamy. Add and blend eggs and vanilla. Mix flour, baking soda, and salt; then mix with cream mixture. Roll dough into quarter size balls and roll in sugar.

Bake at 350° for 8 minutes. Remove from oven and place chocolate kiss in center of each cookie. Bake an additional 2 minutes.

Rum Balls

Ingredients

Makes about 5 dozen

3 cups finely crushed vanilla wafers (about 75)
2 cups powdered sugar
1 cup finely chopped pecans or walnuts
  (about 4 ounces)
1/4 cup cocoa
1/2 cup light rum or bourbon
1/4 cup light corn syrup
Granulated or powdered sugar

Directions

Mix first four ingredients. Stir in rum and syrup. Shape mixture into 1-inch balls and roll in granulated sugar. Cover tightly and refrigerate several days before serving.

Sand Tarts

Ingredients

1 lb soft butter
1 cup powdered sugar
4 cups sifted cake flour
2 cups finely chopped pecans
1 tablespoon vanilla

Directions

Cream together all the ingredients. Chill dough.

Divide dough into tablespoon-size pieces and shape in crescents. Bake 325° for 15–20 minutes or until lightly brown.

Sift powdered sugar. Roll in powdered sugar while still warm.

Snicker Doodle

Ingredients

1 1/2 cups sugar
1/2 cup margarine, softened
1 teaspoon vanilla
2 eggs
2 1/4 cups all-purpose flour
1 teaspoon cream of tartar
1/2 teaspoon soda
1/4 teaspoon salt

For topping:
2 tablespoons sugar
2 teaspoons cinnamon

Directions

Heat oven to 400°.

Combine first four ingredients and blend well. Stir in flour, cream of tartar, soda, and salt. Blend well.

Shape dough into 1 inch balls. Combine sugar and cinnamon. Roll balls in mixture.

Place balls 2 inches apart on ungreased cookie sheet. Bake 8–10 minutes. Immediately remove from cookie sheets.

Sugar Cookies

Ingredients

Makes approximately 7 dozen

2 cups butter

2 cups butter flavored shortening

4 cups sugar

1/8 cup vanilla

1/2 tablespoon and 1/2 teaspoon baking soda

4 eggs

10 cups flour

1/2 cup milk

Directions

Cream butter, shortening, sugar, and vanilla. Add eggs and milk and beat well. Add baking soda and flour and mix well.

Roll into 1-inch balls, or use scoop. Place on ungreased baking sheet and flatten with bottom of a glass dipped in sugar.

Bake at 350° for about 7 minutes.

Cookie dough will freeze well. Serve fresh-baked cookies!

Lemon Bread

Ingredients

Make lemon glaze by cooking the juice and sugar on medium heat until sugar is dissolved. Set aside.

1/3 cup melted butter
2 tablespoons freshly grated lemon peel
1 cup sugar
1 1/2 tablespoons lemon extract
1/2 cup chopped pecans
2 eggs, lightly beaten
1 1/2 cups sifted flour
1 teaspoon baking powder
1 teaspoon salt
1/2 cup milk

Glaze:
1/2 cup fresh lemon juice
1/2 cup sugar

Directions

In a large bowl, mix butter with sugar, lemon extract, and eggs. In a separate bowl, sift flour with baking powder and salt.

To butter mixture, add flour mixture alternately with milk, stirring just enough to blend. Fold in lemon peel and pecans.

Pour batter into greased and floured 9 x 5-inch loaf pan and bake at 350° for 1 hour or until a wooden pick inserted into center comes out clean.

Remove bread from pan and poke holes at 1 inch intervals on all sides. While loaf is still warm, drizzle lemon glaze mixture over top and sides.

Wrap in foil and store for one day before slicing to serve.

A Tribute to Tea and Tea Lovers

Robert Nelson serving holiday tea to guests

DeGolyer Cafe

Camp House

Judith Jenkins

DeGolyer Cafe

Quita Bartholomew

Judy Scott with catering staff

Chef Martin Mendoza

Rutila Balderas

DeGoyler Cafe

Special Memories of Tea

Judy Scott and Barbara Taylor Bradford

In the fall of 2007, a special tea was held for Barbara Taylor Bradford, author of *Woman of Substance*, while promoting her new book, *The Heir*. It was held at the Women's Museum at Fair Park, and four hundred guests attended. My pastry chef, Judith Jenkins, made cookies in the shape of the book and design of the cover. Ms. Bradford was very gracious and delightful.

Another special tea that comes to mind is the Duke and Duchess of Gloucester, Queen Elizabeth's first cousins. We had tea in the spring of 2005 and received very nice compliments from the Duke. He especially liked the scones.

Index